SOUR HONEY & SOUL FOOD

by

billy chapata.

Monarch Publishing, 2017
www.monarchbookstore.com

we go through life **experiencing** so much. tip-toeing our ways through dark mazes, walking steadily on paths filled with cracks and bumps, running aimlessly towards an imaginary finish line that could possibly open up pandora's box.

but nonetheless, we navigate. through clear skies, cloudy days, sunny mornings, and cold nights, we navigate.

sometimes life feels effervescent,

sometimes it feels underwhelming,

sometimes it looks bright,

sometimes darkness surrounds us,

but what is constant is that life is always changing its colors, it's always changing its theme, it's always changing its **flavor**.

we taste everything so closely on the tips of our tongues. the bitter, the sweet, the smooth, the rough:

how does life **taste** to you?

CHAPTERS

SOUR HONEY & SOUL FOOD

robust.

lessons my mother taught me:

open your mind,
before you open your mouth.

patience:

be **patient** with your love, be **wise** with your love, be **affirmative** with your love, don't be wasteful. lock it away, hide the key, and place it on a shelf somewhere in your heart. wait for someone with gentle hands to unlock it. someone who understands your worth, understands your love, understands what you have to offer, and understands that your soul deserves something true. something that doesn't fade after a few trials and stumbles. something that overcomes all obstacles and lasts forever. something **real.**

(respect my space)

my space is **sacred**.
these walls around my
mind are **fragile**.
all i ask is that you
take your shoes off and
wipe your feet before
you enter my mind.
i don't need your dirt.

(there is no need to hold onto something that holds you back from growing. there is no use in holding onto something that stops you from moving forward. there is no use in grasping onto something that destroys your joy and takes away your sanity)

murder the **past**.

(conversations with myself)

dear self,
what?
you were right.
oh, i know.
really?
yeah, you should listen to me more.
i will, i promise.
don't promise, **just do**.

(lessons from my ex)

i will be grateful to you forever,
because you taught me that you can't
force someone to feel.
you taught me that you can't
reciprocate what doesn't exist.
but above all,
you taught me how to **love myself.**

(a few things about that woman)

that's the thing about her. her heart broke, but her mind did not crumble. her heart bled heavily on certain nights, but her mind remained intact, and her soul remained pure. she was **resilient**, she was **strong**, she was stubborn, she was pain, she was **joy**, she was **life**.

bang, bang

your mouth is a gun
and
your words are bullets.
shoot wisely.

(things heartache taught me)

the scars that cannot be visibly seen hurt the most,
the scars that cannot be visibly seen take the longest to heal.
so i will take my time with my healing,
because my heart **deserves** relief,
and my mind **deserves** peace.

(you taught me that words mean nothing if actions don't resonate. now i'm stuck with your words, and you're stuck with my heart)

the sweet words and broken
promises ring in my head
like a broken record, in an
empty liquor store.
i don't resent you,
i don't hate you,
i just wish i had my heart back.

(thank you, for letting me swim in your...mind)

you get to know her, and slowly, you start to realize that her mind is
a beautiful ocean. the **deeper** you dive in,
the more **breathless**
you become.

the yin & yang of conversation.

i. conversations are more than just an exchange of words, syllables and nuances, they are an exchange of energy. you need to be cautious and aware of who you share them with.

ii. text messages are superficial conversations. preset responses misconstrue or sensationalize words so it's hard to gauge what is natural, and also difficult to interpret what is true.

iii. conversations should leave you feeling fulfilled, enlightened or motivated. don't talk, just to talk. let it be worth your time.

- don't let meaningless conversations become a habit. **don't feed your soul half cooked meals.**

clairvoyant caves.

life is like
an echo.

what you send out
comes back,
what you sow
you reap,
what you give
you get,
what you see in others
is in **you**.

(text messages and conversations with the universe)

when you find
that the same
thing keeps
being removed
from your life,
let go,
stop chasing.
it's a **sign**.

(take pride in all the things you've gone through. take pride in them because they have shaped you into the beautiful creation that you are now)

your scars tell **beautiful stories.**

envy.

i find myself missing you sometimes.
wondering what you're doing,
what you're looking at,
what scents surround the air in the place that you're in.
but in all honesty,
it's your tattoos i'm jealous of.
they get to be with you everywhere you go.

3 things i've learnt about a woman's love.

i. when a woman loves;
her love never
wavers. it remains
consistent and true,
even through dark
and troubling times.

ii. when a woman loves;
her love can be
so strong, that it overwhelms
the presence of everything
and everyone around her,
including herself.

iii. when a woman loves;
her eyes never wander.
the attraction of others is
never strong enough to pull
her away from what her
heart desires.

(work on understanding yourself, knowing yourself, freeing yourself. when you have grasped your true essence, outer forces can never compromise your growth)

who you **know** you are
is more important than
who they **think** you are.

(we were made for each other, temporarily)

perhaps, when we first met we were both **broken**.
perhaps, our **scars** are what attracted us to each other.
perhaps, we saw so much similarity in each other that we couldn't resist each other's energy.
perhaps this was the universe's plan to help us find worth in ourselves again, and now that we have fixed each other, we have no use for each other any more.

revelations about women #1

passionate;

passionate women often find themselves struggling to convey love. the flame that burns within them is one that doesn't have an on and off switch. it just exists. their love is so **fierce** that it often gets **misunderstood**.

reserved;

a quiet woman, is sometimes the strongest and the **wisest**. the most underestimated kind of woman. the mysterious woman that no one knows much about. the woman that accomplishes her goals in **silence**. what a reserved woman loses in speech, she gains in lessons and observation.

spiritual;

a true **goddess**. a woman that is one with herself and one with the universe. a woman that makes you feel whole. a woman that prays for you when you least know it. she **empowers** you, and together you can overcome any obstacles that come across your path.

(trying to live in the moment more. trying to find beauty in the now)

we spend too much
time fighting with
clocks, instead of
just enjoying our time.

(keep blossoming, darling)

i see **flowers** growing
from the cracks in your
heart. it's **beautiful**.

(i find women to be very elemental beings, very different and unique in their nature)

fire;
an impulsive woman, short tempered at times. passionate, sexy. lights up
the atmosphere and gives energy to everything she touches.

water;
a laid back woman, very relaxed. smooth, delicate, but destructive when
angered. goes with the flow and others radiate towards that.

wind;
a woman of transition, a free spirit. bipolar, misunderstood and unfazed.
sweet to those that love her, deadly to those that don't.

earth;
a wise woman, a pillar of strength. rich in knowledge and a great support
system. mentally tough, selfless and often taken for granted.

- some women, **are all four.**

(only the universe knows)

maybe,

i was just attracted
to the fact that you're
a hopeless romantic,

perhaps,

i was naive to think
i could teach you
how to love.

the complexities of love.

at times, we invest so much in trying to understand the depths and actions of others, that we lose sight of who we are in the process.

you can't truly love and understand someone without giving them a part of you. it's a sacred exchange, one **you may lose** at times.

but you **can't be afraid** of losing. **you lose, you learn**. that is the beauty of life, and the complexities of love.

deadly.

do not be fooled by her quiet
demeanor. inside her mind there
are **wolves** waiting patiently,
ready to devour anything
that comes their way.

revelations about women #2

i find women that guard their hearts to be intriguing. the **stories** behind their heartbreak are often the **realest** and most soul **captivating**.

equally, there is something alluring about a woman shrouded in **mystery**. the lure of discovering something beautiful **seduces the senses.**

digital vampire.

yes,
when the moon comes out i do
wonder about you at times,
but then i remember
the teeth marks you left on my
soul the last time we spoke.

- i will **not** be calling you anytime soon.

(there was something electrifying about her as she walked into the room. she didn't re-quire speech to captivate, she didn't require speech to be memorable)

i like a woman who lets her **energy speak.**
the kind that walks into a room and illuminates
everything around her without saying a word.

explore your core and your essence.

explore your **darkness** and **light**. what causes you to feel lost and what gives you hope?

explore your **balance**. what causes you to lose it and what anchors your soul when the tides turn?

explore your **aura**. what heightens your mood, what deflates it? what ignites your soul, what makes your heart cold?

explore your **anatomy**. your bumps, your scars. your crevices, your curves. what make your bones quiver, what electrifies your mind?

explore your **friendships** and **relationships**. are you growing from them? or are you stagnating? are you adjusting? or are you settling?

explore your **ego**. what feeds it? what destroys it? how do you contain it and how does it manifest?

explore your **mind**. what makes it tick? what makes it stop? what expands your senses? what takes away your sanity?

explore your **heart**. look at the scars and bruises. are they healing or still painful? what reopened the wound? what closed it?

- learn yourself. learn your scars. **grow.**

(i want to discover the layers that people seem to ignore. the layers you don't like to expose to the rest of the world. the layers that you hide because no one will accept your intricacies)

i don't like
transparency.
i want to discover
hidden treasures within you,
unlock certain doors,
swim in your soul
and test the waters.

(drinking and playing games of "have you ever")

have you ever felt a **connection** with someone?
not in lust or in their image,
but in the richness of their soul,
and the vibes they give off?

(she told me that all of her love fell in the wrong hands)

perhaps,

your mother should have taught you how to **love yourself first**,
instead of how to love a man.

<u>she's divine:</u>

what's
beautiful about
her, is that she
doesn't have
a **crown** on her
head, but you
can tell she's
a **queen** by the
divinity in her soul.

messages in a bottle (take whatever you need)

lost message:

your soul deserves something real. stop allowing people with poisonous energy into your life.

lost message:

you can leave when you desire. it's never too late to take the key out of their pocket and unlock your happiness.

lost message:

own your actions and own your words. do not apologize for what you feel is true. you are not an apology, so why live like one?

lost message:

you are a goddess, you are art. why are you letting these vandals spray paint graffiti all over your soul?

lost message:

it's okay to feel uneasy about your situation right now. a few steps out of your comfort zone will be pivotal to your growth.

lost message;

don't let your kindness breed naivety. you want your soul to be wholesome,
you don't want it to be a doormat.

lost message;

don't let the past dictate you. keep loving like a tidal wave and eventually
you'll find someone who already knows how to swim.

lost message;

you are a book with several chapters. you can rewrite yourself as many times
as you need, remember that.

lost message;

your growth will often be misunderstood by others. they will call accuse you
of changing, and being different. but it's okay, carry on.

lost message;

you're a mystery, and that is beautiful. some will try to shape you into things
only they can understand. you don't have to let them.

(the key to her heart, the combination to her soul)

it's not about writing a poem for her,
it's about making her **feel** like one.

baby steps.

darling,
learn how to walk
into people's lives,
without walking
out of your own.

i've always found trees to be very symbolic in the way they embody certain women's characteristics:

roots; a selfless woman, a support system. the type of woman that values growth and keeps you grounded during times of need.

trunk; a strong woman, a protector. the type of woman that is tested countless times but never wavers. relentless, resilient, divine.

branch; a resourceful woman, a creator. this is the kind of woman that gives life to anything she touches and finds a way out of nothing.

leaves; a vibrant woman, a rare soul. this is the kind of woman that stands out from the crowd, simply because of the divinity she possesses.

soul museums.

the ones that paint your soul, making it more vibrant.
those are the ones you want around,
the ones that bring out the beautiful **art** in you.

(my kind of woman)

she was sexy.
not in the way her body or curves looked,
but in the way her **mind** and **soul** worked.

(do you see how beautifully unattached she is? do you see how unchained her spirit is?)

she doesn't belong to anyone and i think that's the most divine
thing about her.
she's found love within herself and **she's complete alone.**

know yourself.

know your **truth**.
even if it sounds foreign to them.
let the words that roll off your tongue be reminiscent of what's true in you.

know your **peace**. even if they misunderstand.
if you have to be silent, ignore or keep to yourself so be it.
do what gives your soul peace.

know your **environment**.
observe more, listen more and take in more.
don't be oblivious to your surroundings. don't let them use it against you.

know your **worth**.
even if they forget or choose to ignore.
don't let people's perceptions of you, spoil your own perception. you are divine.

(find comfort in yourself first, be the pillow and blanket you crave)

the problem with finding peace in someone else,
is that you give them the power to cause chaos within you as well.
so emancipate yourself, liberate yourself,
find that peace in yourself.

bilingual.

silence is a language
she speaks so well.

(i hope you choose to take the leap with me)

we're just two **naked minds**,
and there is a deep ocean between us.
hopefully we'll be brave enough to swim one day and meet each other half
way.

saccharine.

unforgettable.

i have come across many women in my lifetime. women with alluring eyes, and amazing smiles. women with lovely bodies, and endless curves. i have come across women from all walks of life, that have the exteriors of a goddess. but the women that always remain the most memorable to me, are the women with beautiful minds. the women who cause mind orgasms and stimulate every part of my soul. the women who have plenty of layers to their soul and get more beautiful as you unpeel the surface. the women you can have a conversation with about ideas, spirituality and art at 3 o'clock in the morning. the women who can feed your soul effortlessly and share their energy unselfishly. the women who have stories to tell about love, **heartache** and **growth**. the women with more to them than meets the eye. a beautiful face will keep me intrigued for a short time, but a beautiful mind will keep me intrigued forever.

(you are much more, darling. much more)

don't let your outer shell define your soul.
you are more than your beauty, your shape and your curves.
you need to believe that.

(my kind of woman)

i like women who are **indefinable**.
the kind of woman that keeps you coming back to discover more about her.
the kind of woman with plenty of **layers** to her soul.
the kind that gets even more beautiful with time.
a woman like this, gives me **life**.

(life is not a hollywood movie baby girl, stop running away from emotions and allow yourself to feel)

she told me that
love is a loaded
gun that she's
been trying to
dodge for many
years now.

(change is good)

it's okay to destroy parts of you to **recreate** yourself again.

**to whom this may concern;**

you deserve someone
who will look at
you like a **muse**.
someone who will
pick your crown up
and put it back on
your head when it slips off.

(patience, darling)

be patient.
find love in the roots of your soul,
in the flowers blooming in the cracks of your heart,
find love in yourself first.

messages in a bottle (take what you need, again)

lost message;

your love may not be suitable for everyone, but that's okay. love until some-
one can catch the strong waves that you give off.

lost message;

not everyone's love is suitable for you. that doesn't make you selfish. you
know what you want and deserve. that's beautiful.

lost message;

it's okay to feel lost, confused, misunderstood. it's okay start over. it's okay
to try and rediscover yourself again.

lost message;

stop seeking comfort in the same hands that destroyed you. don't you think
your heart has been broken enough times already?

lost message;

some people are temporary. people grow, evolve and change. stop holding
yourself accountable for failed relationships.

lost message;

it's okay to keep to yourself and hold your peace. not everyone needs to know why you feel the way you feel. just feel.

lost message;

you spend so much time pouring yourself out. leave some of you for yourself.

lost message;

learn to exist when you are unwanted. don't lose sense of your beauty because no one is constantly telling you that you're beautiful.

lost message;

you have a habit of seeing the goodness in others and this is not a bad thing. just know when to leave the bad alone.

lost message;

remember, you can always let go of something that is hurting you to make room for something that will make you feel good.

yourself.

seek yourself,
find yourself,
understand yourself,
love yourself,
know yourself.

(they don't quite understand her, but i think i do)

to the world,
she seems
cold hearted.
she has so
much love to
give, but hasn't
found a soul
that **deserves it.**

**to whom this may concern;**

those memories you hold onto are poisonous, and until you can learn to let
go, you will never fully **heal.**

(you deserve happiness)

sometimes we bottle things in and we don't understand that keeping things in, causes us more pain and suffering. we keep this dripping vile of poison on the doors of our soul, thinking that whatever it is can be held in, and doesn't need to be addressed. but that feeling, lingers and lingers. knocking, and knocking. frustrating you, angering you, saddening you. reminding you of something that you're not trying to revisit, or something you would rather forget. find your release, find your freedom, liberate yourself. sing, write, paint, converse, dance, find a conducive way to turn that pain into growth, and turn your clouds into sunny days. release all that poison to make way for something beautiful. **you deserve happiness.**

(to the woman with a heart filled with confusion)

love shouldn't tear you down and leave you missing pieces,
it should leave you **whole** and improve the pieces you have already.

(please)

learn to let go.
if a connection has withered away, embrace it.
you can't water a dead flower and expect it to grow again.
just **let go**.

(don't mind her, she's glowing)

her vibe is **attractive**.
people think she's stuck in her own little world
but i like the fact that all she cares about is her own happiness.

the thing about her:

it's not even about how she looks, it's about who she is. you may meet other beautiful women, but there's something unforgettable about her. it could be her aura, her essence, or her vibe, or it could just be the fact that in a world so superficial, she chooses to be herself. that's the most beautiful thing about her. she's unaffected by negativity and the false opinions people may have about her. she just **lives.**

(lessons from the universe)

those that are meant to stay in your life, will stay.
let the others go.
the universe is **rejecting them for a reason**, trust that.

(lessons my mother taught me)

you can't set about trying to prove yourself to people who are **committed to misunderstanding you.** understand yourself, forget the rest.

revelations about women #3

i've learnt that a woman with a broken past needs to be treated with
patience.
she needs time to **breathe**, to **heal**, to **rediscover** herself.
a mistreated woman will reject love countless times before she gives in,
because she's lost sense of what it's like to be treated right.
but the beautiful thing about heartbroken women is the wisdom the past has
given them and the capacity of love they have to offer.
it's endless.

<u>to whom this may concern:</u>

don't force a connection because you're lonely.
don't confuse loneliness with love.
too many connections fade away and relationships fail
because our intentions are led by loneliness instead of substance.
you want someone to fill voids, someone to cure the sadness, someone to
stop the pain.
it doesn't begin with anyone else, it **begins with you.**
when you love when you're lonely, you place all your happiness in that per-
sons hands.
when they're gone, your happiness goes with them.
choose love for yourself.

messages in a bottle (take what you need, once more)

lost message:

if they can only love you in pieces, they will never truly appreciate you when you are whole.

lost message:

you are art. you deserve to be appreciated, loved and adored. you deserve to be remembered. you deserve to be someone's muse.

lost message:

that door to the past you keep trying to re-open has nothing new. tear up that old map, and draw a new one. move on.

lost message:

you're a fire and a hurricane all in one. one person may not be able to handle your passion and love, but someone else will.

lost message:

it's time to distance yourself from the people who let you down, the inconsistent ones. it's time to start loving yourself.

lost message:

stop spilling your thoughts to people who don't want to see you grow. stop sharing your emotions and feelings with deaf ears.

lost message:

people keep telling you who to love and when to love, but there's nothing wrong with loving the only way you know how.

lost message:

things are rough right now, but that smile on your face never fades away. you're much stronger than they know. i admire that.

lost message:

darkness is not a bad thing. your journey will have rainy days, and quiet nights, but this time is so key to your growth.

lost message:

on some days you feel everything and on other days you feel nothing at all. life changes. embrace that change, learn from it.

(she encompasses much more than the ordinary)

she loves like
no other.
she loves like
a **sister**,
a **mother**
and a **best friend.**
lose her love
and you'll feel
like you've lost
a part of yourself.

(evolve, and never look back)

you're not required to be the person you were yesterday.
evolve.
don't be ashamed of your growth.
don't feel guilty for outgrowing people.

(she's a work of art, don't you see?)

she's the type you don't have to write about.
she's the type you just observe and admire from a far
because everything she does is **poetry**.

their loss.

you're a work in progress.
some people won't be patient enough with you while you grow.
remember, they're missing out, not you.

heal softly:

don't rush your healing process.
let your heart **breathe**,
let your wounds **mend**,
and **rediscover** yourself slowly.
let your healing process be beautiful and fruitful.
learn about yourself,
learn about others.
learn what to accept and reject in the future.

(lessons my ex taught me)

some people don't know what to do with love. you could give them all the love in the world, and they may not accept it, they may ignore it, or they may just not know how to handle it. i've learnt not to take it personally, but above all, i've learnt that not everyone is suitable for what you have to offer, and that **not everyone is suitable** for your love.

(an angel with a vicious tongue)

her words were
smooth and sweet
on some days,
and hard to swallow
on others.
she was like a spoon
full of **honey**,
with a shot of **vodka**.

messages in a bottle (take what you need, darling)

lost message:

you're their safe haven. they come to you when they're lonely, lost or bored. distance yourself, you're worth more than that.

lost message:

being accepted by someone who loves you should be effortless. don't be forced into doing things that makes your soul unhappy.

lost message:

you're beautiful. understand that without the validation of another human being, and that beauty will last forever.

lost message:

are you really happy giving out so much with nothing in return?

lost message:

the pain is deep, you don't let many in. some may not understand this, but only you can understand your own healing process.

lost message:

solitude is good sometimes. you can't fly when you're constantly surrounded by people who cut off your wings.

lost message:

there's nothing wrong with living for yourself at times. there's nothing wrong with being a little selfish and focusing within.

secrets about me:

i've got too much **passion** in my bones
and too much **fire** in my soul to love half-heartedly.
you either get it all, or get nothing at all.

<u>soul marks.</u>

it's the ones that have seen you at your worst,
but accept your imperfections,
that **tattoo** themselves on your soul
and become **unforgettable**.

short poem to my ex:

i hope you find what
you're looking for.
but if you never do,
just know that i'll be
long gone by then.

so much love, so much.

you need to love yourself.
love yourself so much to the point that
your energy and aura **rejects** anyone
who doesn't know your worth.

let me say my peace:

silence is an intriguing thing. the funny thing about silence is how easily it is misinterpreted. no, i am not anti-social. no, i am not avoiding anyone. no, i am not upset, sad or angry. i am just silent. my silence is a statement, my silence is my peace of mind, my silence is **poetry**.

inner glow.

a woman who knows that her beauty resonates within,
will always be more **powerful** than a woman
who lets her outer beauty speak for her.

**chapters on chapters:**

there are beautiful
poems stored in
your scars,
and sometimes
it takes the right
person to **reveal**
all of the **pages**.

(there is nothing that intrigues me more than the journey that brought people to the place they are at now. what happened? what transpired? why did those events take place?)

i like a woman with a past. a woman with a story to tell. **stories** of pain, heartbreak and joy. stories that shaped her into what she is today.

free:

the goal is not to drown them in love. it's to give them love they can dive in, come up for air, and swim freely in. a **boundless** kinda' love.

miss-understood.

she's art.
you don't have to understand her.
she wasn't built to validate your opinion.
accept her for the **beautiful ambiguity** that she is.

(your insecurities, have nothing to do with me)

people hate it when you know your worth. you draw the line, you set the precedence, you stand your ground, and they flip the coin on you and make it seem like you're the one with a problem. "you're too demanding, you're too selective, you're too judgmental, you're too unrealistic". no, i'm neither of those things. **i just love myself.** i love myself enough to know what i need, what will improve me, what will grow me, what i deserve. i'm loving myself, and there is absolutely nothing wrong with that.

to whom this may concern;

don't let this world turn you cold. don't let the pain harden your heart. these bad times will **grow** you.

(lessons about women)

a woman won't allow everyone to **undress** her soul.
but if you get the chance to do so,
she's letting you know that she wants you to stay.

(to the woman who loves hard, and loves with everything in her soul)

i hope your love is always reciprocated, and if it isn't, i hope you find the **strength** to walk away.

rules to love.

there are no rules to love. no limitations, no boundaries, no restrictions, no inhibitions. you could fall in love with someone after many years, or fall in love with them after a few days. you could fall in love with someone you have much in common with, or someone who is not similar to you at all. but that's the beauty of love. the indefinable nature of it all leaves room for the growth of something beautiful. something that can be understandable at times, or something that can be ambiguous or confusing on some occasions. there is no right or wrong way to fall in love, neither is there a right or wrong way to love. create your own happiness, create your own definitions, **create your own** rules of love.

potential lover:

we can fall in love without destroying each other.
we can fall in love without having to change a single thing about one anoth-
er.

unfazed.

listen to how
she laughs
even through
the tough times.
notice how all
the pain and
burden don't
weigh her
smile down.

(leave her wild)

let her bloom naturally.
don't change her into a flower you saw in someone else's garden.
water her when she needs it, but let her be.

(you're beautiful the way you are. you're amazing the way you are. you're memorable the way you are. these magazines and tv shows create illusions of what is desirable, and i hope you realize that you are much deeper than what the media wants you to see and believe)

i hope you never find the need to diminish your aura
by imitating other things people find beautiful.
i hope you can find divinity **within**.

coincidence.

coincidence? i don't believe in coincidence. that word, doesn't exist in my souls dictionary. there is much more to everything that happens on our journeys. for two souls to cross paths is more than just mere coincidence. to feel a connection unlike anything you've ever felt before isn't by mistake. something brought you to this place. something wants you to be in this place. a beautiful story could be on the verge of taking place.

<u>to my unborn daughter:</u>

the beauty you seek,
is not in magazines,
movies and books.
the beauty you seek resonates within **you.**

zest.

beautifully hidden.

see,
she's beautiful,
but there's much
more to her.
so many layers
she has hidden.
layers she hides
because few deserve
her sacredness.

(*she's got magic in her*)

her thighs are a place of divinity,
and if she lets you in,
it's enough to make you feel **godly**.

**lessons about women:**

if a woman is passionate about something, **let her be.** if you have to dim her light because you can't handle it, she probably isn't for you.

appreciate a woman's passion while it still exists. **cherish it, embrace it.** when a woman loses her passion for you, there's no restoring it.

useless titles.

what are we? is that important? do we need a title to define our connec-
tion? does the lack of a label make our connection less important? less
meaningful? less beautiful? does a connection need to have a title to have
sustenance? or is it the actions within the connection that breed longevity?
"boyfriend, girlfriend, husband, wife, boo, bae", it makes no difference. we
don't really need to know what we are, as long as we have a mutual under-
standing for each other and a love that can't be broken by outer forces. **a
connection deeper than just titles**, legal connotations and cute nicknames.
a connection between two beautiful souls who have every intention of grow-
ing with each other and conquering the world together.

(breathe)

breathe a little.
don't let life consume you.
don't miss out on life because you're inhaling too much of it.
exhale and cherish the moments.

**text messages and conversations with the universe:**

what is for you, will come naturally.
you will find no need to force it,
no need to stress it,
it will just **flow**.

*(you are worth much more than someone's uncertainty and doubt. you are worth affir-
mative intentions. you are way too divine to be holding onto someone who doesn't want
to hold on to you)*

progress.
grow.
elevate yourself.
there is no time to be waiting around for someone who is still knocking on
doors from the past.

consistent lover.

some women light fires in your soul and leave,
other women light a torch up,
hold it firm and ensure that fire never goes out.

be appreciated.

be appreciated. i mean, be really appreciated. strive for something befitting your worth. don't let anyone else dictate it, only you have the right and power to do that. your warmth does not deserve to be greeted with coldness, your sincerity does not deserve to be met with ambiguity, and your love is not meant to be met with anything other than love. you're worth more than mixed signals, more than half-hearted words, and more than inconsistent actions. **be appreciated.** be really, appreciated.

(lessons my ex taught me)

i've found comfort
in empty hearts before,
it's the loneliest place
your love can reside.

**to whom this may concern;**

i know it must be difficult to be a strong and attractive woman in a world that bases its merits of validation on likes, retweets and comments. your beauty and depth is minimized by people's perceptions of image and the social construct that media has emphasized upon us all. people can't quite grasp the other layers that make you the truly unique and divine woman that you are. they can't see how vast your mind is by looking at your body, they can't see how intellectual you are by looking at your face, and they can't absorb your true essence just by seeing the outer characteristics you encompass. you are more than your body, your face and your curves. you are a **goddess** with much more to you, and always remind yourself of that.

you deserve;

someone who's crazy about you.
someone whose presence **improves** your inner being.
someone whose passion for you is not hidden.

(when the timing is right, you can let that ship sail)

some thoughts are meant to be free,
and some thoughts are meant to be handcuffed to the frame of your mind
until the **time is right.**

<u>*listen:*</u>

she's **learning** to love herself,
be **patient** with her.

(your weak days don't define you)

it's okay to have days when you feel weak. days when your bones cannot sustain the weight and pressure the world has put on your shoulders. days when you can't mentally grasp the essence of everything around you. days when you want to just roll up in a small cocoon to avoid everyone and their energy. days when you just want to float away somewhere on a cloud to escape reality. days when the only feeling that makes sense, is a feeling of retreat. you are not defined by your weak moments. feel what you feel, and keep a sticky note inscribed with beautiful words somewhere at the back of your mind, to remind yourself that everything is **temporary**.

**jackpot.**

be with someone who recognizes that there is gold in your soul,
but doesn't dig it out.
someone who lets you **shine** unapologetically.

(on the phone with a person called infatuation)

it was the idea of me that fascinated you. looking into the window of my soul from the outside, you saw something you didn't need, but something you wanted. and just like everything we get that we want, the appeal and charm wore off over time, and the intrigue i presented ended. you got a taste of my reality and what the world i encompass presents but it didn't match the mental art piece you obsessed over for so long. now you're just a **stranger**, and i'm just a prisoner of your infatuation.

letters to royalty:

queen;
when did you start clothing yourself in the false opinions of others, and leaving the clothes you like at home? when did you start obsessing about the smiles on other people's faces while neglecting the one on your own? why do you sleep with your demons every night and wonder why tranquility and peace eludes you? what happened to the beautiful queen that held her crown high when days were dark? i hope you find the answers, and **find yourself again.**

king;
when did you handcuff yourself to the idea that vulnerability is a weakness? when did searching for temporary highs become more appealing than finding something that nourishes your soul for an eternity? why does the impression you have on your peers matter more than the impression you leave on yourself? why does the search for riches concern you when it makes you feel emptier than fulfilled? i hope you find the answers, and **find yourself again.**

(she's becoming my drink of choice)

sip **slowly**. a few tastes of her and you'll never be the same again.

new, you.

i heard you were
focusing a little
more on yourself,
and worrying a
little less about
everyone else.
it's **beautiful**.

remember:

peace of mind in exchange for love, is **never a fair trade.**

(the secret to life)

once you understand that you don't need to be in love to be happy,
you'll stop searching and accepting things you don't **deserve**.

no fault of her own.

they say that she's absorbed in her own essence, i say it's beautiful that she is. it's beautiful that she's focused on her own journey, it's beautiful that all she's concerned about is her growth, it's beautiful that she doesn't follow the crowd and does her own thing. she's a free spirit, going with the wind, and if you can't keep up with her, that's no fault of her own.

a delightful paradox:

she could be hell
on some days,
heaven on others,
sunny on some days,
gloomy on others,
you had to experience
both to understand
her **beauty**.

**limited availability.**

it's beautiful how she's
only available to few.
how she only reveals herself
to those that appreciate her colorful **petals**.

(let it happen)

with time, your soul will outgrow certain things.
the clothing that once kept your soul warm
will stop fitting and you will need a **change**.

(be weary of the people you let in. the people you decide to trust. the people you decide to put your faith in. feel their energy, learn it, understand it, and decide whether they have your best interests at hand)

sometimes the most **poisonous** people,
come in the form of **medicine**.

3 little gems i picked up from failed relationships:

i. **connection** with yourself is more important than one you can have with anyone else. don't destroy yourself to make someone else whole.

ii. there is no harm in **patience**. don't be rushed into being something you're not, by souls that don't appreciate your growth and being.

iii. sometimes life will leave you in the middle of the ocean with no one around you, but that doesn't mean you should **stop** swimming.

understand:

no, i don't need you to complete me. i don't need your presence to make me feel whole. there may be days when i'm alone, but that doesn't mean i'm lonely. there may be days when i'm silent, but that isn't a plea for attention. the idea of being loved doesn't fascinate me as much as the idea of loving myself. until i find a connection that makes sense to my heart, and a connection that resonates with my soul, i'm fine on my **own**.

about her:

very few have
seen her with
no clothes on,
even fewer have
seen her mind **naked**.

<u>an angel with horns.</u>

a quiet woman,
with a naughty mind.
she doesn't search
for late night adventures,
she brings late night
adventures to you.

(she was a different kind of woman. diamonds and pearls didn't really appeal to her. she was far from your ordinary)

she wasn't a woman fascinated by materialism and tangible things.
she was lured by beautiful and memorable experiences.
she wanted to **feel**.

**to whom this may concern;**

i know you crave deep conversation.
you don't have to dumb yourself down
to suit other people's **intellectualism.**

best of both.

on some days
she's the blunt,
on some days
she's the ashtray,
on other days
she's the flame that
creates and destroys.

(the simple things)

i love conversations where you can bounce energy off each other. i water you, you water me, we grow **mentally** and **spiritually** together.

ruined.

i hate the fact that they told you how beautiful you are. not because it isn't true, but only because they used it as a way to get closer to you. a shower of compliments that made you feel unique, made your soul glow, and made your heart feel safe. only to turn around and hurt you with poisonous actions that don't fit all the sweet words. i hate the fact that they told you that you're beautiful, because when i tell you that you are, you remember the last time you were called beautiful, and feel the opposite.

(there is distance between us, but it's not for the lack of caring)

loving from a distance doesn't make the love less potent.
admiring a flower from afar without
plucking it from the ground allows it to **grow**.

(if you don't intend to love every part of her, don't love her at all)

and when you love her,
love her stretch marks,
love her scars,
love her bruises,
love her imperfections,
love **every part** of her.

(now that she is firmly in your life)

be **gentle** with her,
she's been broken before.

(to the woman with tears in her eyes and a broken heart)

you fell in love
and immediately
fell out of love
with yourself.
that's when i
knew the one
you love, wasn't
loving you the
way you **deserve**.

(i've learnt to take you in small quantities)

she was the
type of woman
you had to take
in **small doses**,
because her aura
was **addictive**.

**questions.**

when was the last time you let your soul **breathe**
and stopped stressing about the things you can't control?

(have you been lucky enough to indulge?)

every woman has **chapters** in her soul that she lets few read,
deep **oceans** that she lets few swim in,
hidden **mazes** that only few have escaped.

epiphanies:

i used to think that all i needed was someone that makes me happy. someone that makes me smile, someone that makes me laugh, someone that makes me feel good. but happiness is a temporary feeling, it comes and goes. anyone can make you happy, anyone can make you smile, anyone can make you laugh, but very few people can truly understand you. very few people can truly resonate with your soul and see deeper things than how they appear on the surface. very few people see beyond, the smiles, the laughs and the goodness. very few people understand that there is more to love than happiness. maybe it's not a case of being with someone who makes you happy, but being with someone who will be there for you even when you're not.

(keep your crown up)

there is life after failed connections,
there is love after failed connections.
it's not the end,
but just the **beginning** and **rebirth**
of something new.

love journey.

your love will be
misunderstood,
your love will be
taken for granted,
your love will go
through trials before
it finds a **home**.

late night cravings:

physical attraction was
not what stimulated her.
she craved someone who
could undress her mind
with words, someone
who found her **mind** sexy.

<u>a tragic masterpiece.</u>

she's a beautiful mess.
she'll pick up all the
broken pieces
she lost from herself,
and find a way to
recreate herself again.

notes on healing:

our healing process only begins when we allow ourselves to be vulnerable. when we stop running from our pain and hiding in the shadows of denial. sometimes we inhibit our healing process by trying too hard to heal. your healing process can never be forced, it is a natural process that happens over a period of time. it's a process that takes self love, patience, and acceptance. it's okay to have lingering feelings for someone who hurt you, it's okay to be stuck and confused emotionally, it's okay to close in and focus on yourself. you are not a robot, your feelings were not meant to be premeditated, your feelings were not meant to be understood by everyone. allow yourself to grow, allow yourself to breathe, allow yourself to feel, allow yourself to **heal.**

i urge you;

never to settle. there is **more** out there. more oceans to swim in, more clouds to sleep in, more energy and vibrations to feel.

<u>*confidante.*</u>

when a woman shows
you her dark side,
there is a certain light
in you that she sees.
a certain **light** she doesn't
see in anyone else.

(*her beauty is in her strength. how she puts her heart out there, and still recovers after she suffers heartbreak*)

you thought the pain you
caused her would hinder
her growth.
you thought the pain you
caused her would change
her for the worst.
but the love she
never received from you,
gave her the courage to
love herself.

- the only person who lost, is you.

(the trick to comprehending her)

sometimes,
the best way
to understand
her, is to
understand
her **silence.**

piquant.

<u>uncharted territory:</u>

homes are not
always buildings,
places, countries.
sometimes **homes
are people**, with
locked doors and
fences to stop
anyone from coming in.

her:

the thing about her, is that she was happy alone. everyone around her was looking for a connection and something to grasp onto, but she was happy being free. she was happy being unchained, happy with no pressure of connections and love. all the love she needed was within herself, and everybody else was just a distraction from everything she was trying to achieve. she understood herself more than anyone else understood her, and that was the most **beautiful** thing about her.

impulses.

never be afraid to express yourself,
and never find shame in holding your tongue
when silence speaks better for you.

(i feel lucky)

have you ever seen her at her most **vulnerable**?
when her soul has no make-up on?
she only shows few, but that's when she's most beautiful.

you have license.

you are allowed to evolve and leave the past behind.
you are allowed to leave the roots that held you for so long
and **plant yourself elsewhere.**

(she's got that aaliyah, lauryn, lisa left eye, sade, erykah, kinda' vibe)

she reminds me of
90's r&b and sun
kissed sunflowers.
she's the woman
you can't get off
your mind, and
the woman you
think of in the future.

you are much more:

you are not your past. you are not the pain you've suffered. you are not your scars. you are not the mistakes you've made. you are not your weak moments. you are not your failed connections. you are not people's opinions. you are not the false idea people conjure up in their head, you are more than that. you are more beautiful than that. you are more intricate than that. you are more divine than that. you are more valuable than that. you are more exquisite than that. you are more than what people think, feel or say. **you are much more.**

as you please;

you are allowed to
be hot on some days
and cold on others.
you're allowed to
flow like lava and
crash like the ocean.
you are allowed to feel.

(you want to be loved by a woman who loves herself. you want to be loved by a woman who cherishes her own existence and is not defined by anyone)

a woman who loves,
is powerful.
a woman who loves
herself,
is **unstoppable.**

chameleon soul.

she was constantly
evolving. every time
they thought they
understood her,
she added a new color
or texture to the art
piece she already is.

**a walking contradiction;**

fire in her bones,
honey in her soul.
she's **sweet** when
she has to be,
and **fierce** when
she needs to be.

to whom this may concern;

if they can only appreciate you in pieces,
say your **peace, collect** yourself,
and **appreciate** yourself the way
you deserve to be appreciated.

(she doesn't waste time, and you should've known better)

she's a woman
who doesn't spend
time in spaces that
don't **celebrate** her.
you can't choose
when to love her.
you either do,
or she's gone.

know the love you deserve;

love should be a home, that you can come back to. a sanctuary that makes you feel safe, feel comfortable, feel unjudged. once you start to feel the opposite of those emotions, perhaps the place you once called home, is not the place you should be resting your heart at every night. too often, we accept love that comes in beautiful, shiny bottles. love that looks good on the outside, but tastes sour and displeasurable on our tongue and soul. we accept it because we feel like deep down, there is nothing better for us. we feel that the love we're receiving is the best we can get. that the "love", doesn't get better than what we're receiving. love is not perfect, by any means, but when reassurance becomes more desirable to you than actually feeling the love you're receiving, then you have to raise the question - am i being loved, the way i need to be loved? there is nothing wrong with wanting to be loved in a way you feel you deserve. it is not selfish, it is not inconsiderate, it is not self centered. it is only a beautiful sign of your self-worth. **know yourself**, and **know the love you deserve.**

darling,

running back to the same hands that broke you, will not **heal** you.

phantom of self-love.

her beauty
drew them in,
but her mind,
scared them away.
they couldn't
handle a woman
with more to her
than just **surface glow**.

text messages and conversations with the universe;

reflect back.
look at how much you've grown.
remove all the dead flowers from your hearts garden and keep **recreating**
yourself.

(your peace of mind and sanity is worth more than any resentment you may hold against someone. let all of it go)

let grudges go. feed your soul **peace** and **honey**. take that backpack full of bitterness off. you deserve to travel **light** on your journey.

**epiphanies about love;**

the word "love", is so misused and so saturated. the meaning of love is lost.
people don't know how it looks, how it tastes, how it feels. somewhere along
the path, where cracked hearts, broken souls and unspoken words lay, the
true meaning of love lives.
seeking,
searching,
perusing.
when will you stop seeking and actually working on a connection through
the faults, speed bumps and hurdles?
love is not just a feeling, it's a choice.
i'm learning this more and more every day.

(waiting for what is meant for me)

i no longer force things.
what **flows, flows.** what **crashes, crashes.**
i only have space and energy for things that are meant for me.

(swallow your pride, and do what you have to do)

ego is the main **killer** of love.

conference call.

to you;

you've left pieces of yourself, with the ones you've loved before, but now it's time to recreate yourself, into something stronger.

to her;

don't let the world make you feel inadequate. your love was meant for those who can swim in deep waters, leave the rest on shore.

to him;

never miss the opportunity to tell her how much you love her. be vulnerable and transparent with her. show her she's a queen.

(love is a risk worth taking)

love is not straightforward. it's like boarding a train in a foreign land, without knowing what the final destination is. taking a leap of faith without knowing whether you'll injure yourself or land safely. trying to unlock a safe without knowing what the combination or sequence is. sometimes the train moves fast, and sometimes the train moves slow. the one constant is that the train is always going somewhere. you can never truly understand or experience the beauty of love until you board that train. so when you find someone worth boarding that train for, love with everything you have, love with everything in your soul - **keep that train moving**.

**paint cans full of rainbows.**

she's a woman who
won't be moulded into
what you want her to be.
she'll grab a paintbrush,
grab the sky, and **create
herself** as she pleases.

(pack your bags, darling)

self love is a **journey**.
it is not something that you will wake up feeling.
it is not instantaneous.
it is something that will take **time**.

(blues for her)

it's your beauty that gets me. heart skipping beats, arms shaking, palms
sweaty, uncontrollable anxiety. your eyes are more fierce than fully loaded
machine guns. effortlessly taking shots right at my chest, i find myself un-
able to breathe and think correctly. it's difficult to comprehend when you're
the shooter, but as the person in front of the barrel, i feel your intensity at
full force. i feel your power, your energy, i feel you. i have tried dodging,
and shielding myself, but no bullet proof vest can deflect your shots or stop
you from penetrating the depths of my soul. not sure if i should consider
myself a victim, or one of the fortunate few to experience you at full capac-
ity and still survive. it's rare to come across such divinity and perfection, so
excuse me if it takes a while to get used to your beauty.

look at her closely:

do you see how she unapologetically
wears her pain, happiness, flaws
and confusion on her skin?
she's **walking poetry.**

darling,

stop holding yourself accountable for failed connections and questioning your love. you're not for everyone and not everything is meant for you.

to the woman.

i appreciate the woman with a healing heart. the woman with a broken past. the woman who has been lied to and cheated on. the woman who has been taken for granted. the woman whose love has been misunderstood. the woman who has been used and mislead. the woman who has placed her energy and warmth in the wrong hands. the woman who has gone through trials and troubles - i appreciate her because she still manages to stand on two feet. she still manages to breathe when the room around her shrinks. she still manages to smile and laugh on cloudy days. she still manages to love even though it's been unrequited. she still manages, to live. that woman, i appreciate her.

**dream lover;**

a lover who you can
travel the world with,
but a lover who can
also find ways to
visit the world that
exists within you.

gold and godly.

you can't afford
a woman like her.
she has too much
gold in her soul.

(my ex lover)

they ran away from
her scars but i found
beauty in them. i wanted
to write poetry on her
skin, and turn her wounds
and bruises into **flowers**.

affirmations.

speak what you want into existence. let the universe hear your thoughts. send messages in the wind. create a mutuality with the universe.

speak **growth** into your life. you deserve to grow from that place of darkness you've been stuck in. you deserve to bloom even in the winter.

speak **love** into your life. you deserve to be loved as much as you love others. your heart deserves to feel the warmth you make others feel.

speak **prosperity** into your life. you deserve to see your dreams come to fruition. you deserve to eat the fruits of your labor and celebrate.

speak **change** into your life. you deserve a life that is flowing, connections that are not stagnant, love that evolves you. change is good.

speak **substance** into your life. your mind and soul deserve to swim in depth. you deserve to be filled with knowledge, love and excitement.

mother tongue.

intuition is my first **language**.
i'm **fluent** in matters of the soul.

victories and losses.

never losing.
even when i think i'm losing something,
i'm gaining in other aspects of my life.
there is **beauty in every loss.**

i hope;

you find a multi-dimensional lover who loves you in different ways. i hope
you find a lover whose love evolves as you evolve too.

(my kind of woman)

she was
multi-dimensional.
she liked **hip-hop**
and **astrology**.
she got lost in the
melodies but she
belonged to the stars.

perhaps;

you should've
paid more attention to
her while her passion
for you still existed. now
she's gone and all her
magic is gone with her.

honeymoon phase.

i've never really known love beyond the honeymoon phase. i've never really known how love tastes when the sweetness melts away. i've never really known how it feels when my flaws are exposed to my other half for the world to behold. i've become accustomed to people running or turning away when my flaws come to the fore. i've become used to people giving up when the waves become too intense to swim in. i've become used to being the last soldier fighting in a battle that was meant for two souls. i still believe in love, i just don't believe in the words. i don't believe in the "i love you's", "i miss you's", and other terms and phrases of endearment. i believe in the actions behind them. i believe in a love that doesn't go missing. i believe in a love that doesn't choose when to be present. i believe in a love that doesn't come with conditions. i believe that i deserve that, and so do you.

darling,

pain does not define you. do not wear it around your neck like jewelry. **choose happiness** even when the world doesn't want you to.

lessons i learnt:

if they don't feel like home,
don't **overstay** your welcome.

more affirmations.

more connections that flow.
less connections that feel like oil and water.
more connections that feel **effortless** and **enriching**.

**darling,**

you were never unlovable,
you were **never too much**,
you were never bothersome.
they just **misunderstood the magic** you come with.

(they asked me how you write poetry for a woman like her? how do you write poetry for a woman who has so many indescribable beautiful characteristics to her? how do you write poetry for a woman who is a poem in her own right?)

how do you write
poetry for a woman
who is a poem already?
you let **her exist, let her be**,
and allow her to write
herself as she pleases.

you no longer have power over me.

you no longer have power over me. you had me in the cusp of your hands, but that is no longer the case. i slipped away slowly and carefully, when the chains seemed to be at their tightest, and now i'm free. at one point it seemed impossible to escape, and my world seemed to be crashing before me, but time has filled in the blank spots and questions i was flooded with. i can think of you now, without getting angry, upset or sad, i can think of you without drowning myself in "what if's" and "if only's", i can think of you without internalizing and wondering what i could have done differently. i dug deep and i discovered something that i had lost when you were in my life - self love. as an extension of that love, i still pray for you, wish you well, send you love from a distance, but i have myself again, and **having myself is more important than having you.**

digest.

life tastes like **sour honey** to me, and the lessons that come are **soul food**. the lessons come in different flavors - sweet on some occasions, bitter on others. but nonetheless, beautiful. grateful for the lessons, grateful for the experiences, grateful for the people who have inspired my growth, grateful for the different flavors the universe has brought to my mind palate.

how does life taste to **you**?